For my Grandchildren
Emily, Brady & Maddie
who have taught me
how to laugh and
be a child again!

©2017 Robin B. Davis. All rights reserved. No part of this book may be reproduced, stored in a retrieval system, or transmitted by any means without the written permission of the author.

ISBN-13: 978-0-692-99014-8

There's a special hat for every head.

The Hat Shoppe, **"A New Hattitude"** was a popular place in downtown Bluemont, Kentucky.

Miss BeeDee and her cousin, **Mister Tanner Jackson**, had been the owners for many years and they knew just about everyone in the town. Colorful hats of all shapes and sizes lined the shelves, glowing and sparkling as the sun moved along the front window of the shop. All of them were lovingly hand-crafted and named by Miss BeeDee, and inside was a small label that read, *"There's a special hat for every head."*

Mr. Tanner was a tailor and had patched up dresses, pants, and jackets that were passed down from child-to-child in local families for many years.

He loved to joke with the kids about the color of the patches.

Early each morning, Miss BeeDee would dust the wooden shelves and re-arrange the hats, calling them by name as she pretended to talk to them. What she did not know was that the hats heard her, and were always talking about the fun happenings in the store. Sawyer, the Straw Hat, would make up funny stories and the others would try to guess which hat the customers would buy. Most hats were happy to be bought by someone special, except Sawyer. He was real sweet on Sadie, the spoon bonnet with the colored flowers, and did not want to leave. Though Sadie was a bit shy, she loved to laugh when Sawyer charmed her with his humor, and wanted to stay with him at the shop.

"**Oh, look Mother, the hat in the corner with the flowers,**" squealed Mallory. "**Isn't it just perfect?**"

"**It's one of my favorites,**" tooted Miss BeeDee proudly, as she walked over to the shelves. "**Her name is Sadie,**" she said as she placed the hat on Mallory's head. Mallory danced around the mirror in the corner of the store, happy as she could be.

"**It's for the Durango Derby next month,**" said Miss Hannah Mason, Mallory's Mom. "**How exciting!**" said Miss BeeDee. Sawyer listened carefully for clues about Sadie's new owner. "**They live at Red Hawk Farm,**" he heard, "**and she will be riding in the Derby.**"

Then, out the door went Mallory with Sadie sitting snugly on her head. Sawyer's heart sank. His long-time sweetheart was gone, and he might never see her again.

Swoosh!!! The door swung open and Miss Sarah walked in with Zeke, her son, who worked at Lickety-Split Stables caring for the horses. "The sun's getting mighty hot this time of year," said Miss Sarah, have you a good hat for Zeke?" "Oh yes, a big brim is what you need," said Miss BeeDee, as she took Sawyer off the shelf and handed it to Zeke. It fit perfectly, and would surely keep the sun out.

"Woo-hoo!" hollered Zeke, "This hat feels like it was made just for me." Miss BeeDee laughed, "There's a special hat for every head!" "Thanks, Miss BeeDee", said Zeke, as he skipped out of the store.

The Hat Shoppe had a beautiful pink glow as the sun began to set and the day came to a close. Miss BeeDee and Mister Tanner packed up their bags and headed home.

"**I'm going to miss Sawyer's stories and jokes,**" said Darby, the Derby. "**Yeah, me too,**" said Brady, the Baseball Cap. "**I miss Sadie too, I loved how she laughed at Sawyer's jokes.**" "**I will tell new stories,**" said Freddie, the Fez. "**You?**" said Parker, the Policeman, as he burst into laughter. "**Yes, we can all do it together.**" said Buddy, the Beany Top. Everyone agreed; the Hat Shoppe would always be a fun place to tell stories, and to enjoy the customers as they came in and out.

Cock-a-doodle-doo... It was dawn at Lickety-Split Stables. Zeke grabbed a biscuit off the kitchen table, and pushed the door open. Bang!!! Mr. Dalton, the head trainer, was already in the stables. **"Hey Zeke,"** he said, **"Miss Hannah Mason wants us to train her daughter Mallory to ride in the Derby. I think "Whistler's Secret" would be the perfect horse for her. What do you think?" "Yes Sir, Mister. Dalton,"** said Zeke, **"that's a fine choice."**

"Had he really heard this?" thought Sawyer, sitting on Zeke's sweaty brow. **"Could it be that Mallory was going to be trained by Mister Dalton at the Lickety-Split Stables?"** Surely, he would get to see Sadie again.

Saturday morning was always lively at the Hat Shoppe. Mister Landon Polk was first in, with Sally, Billy and Tommy Polk. "That one Dad, the one with the tail on it. I'm going to be Daniel Boone!" said Billy. Today was his 6th birthday and this is what he wanted more than anything. "Well, Miss BeeDee, said Mister Landon, he's been talking about that raccoon hat for weeks. Never seen him so excited!"

"**This is Charlie,**" said Miss BeeDee as she pulled it off the shelf. "**Zippity-doo-dah!**" shouted Billy as he danced around in front of the mirror. "**Charlie is my new best friend!**"

Miss BeeDee chuckled, "**I don't think that hat is ever coming off his head!**" "I think you're right," responded Landon. "**Sally, Tommy, let's get home for the party.**" They both grabbed another cookie and off they went. Billy skipped his way around the store and scooted out behind them. "**Thanks, Miss BeeDee!**"

Back at the stables, Mister Dalton was walking "Whistler's Secret" around the ring with Mallory Mason on his back. Mallory had a huge smile on her face and her curly brown hair flowed down to her shoulders, tucked beneath her beautiful bonnet, Sadie!

Zeke rode by on one of the other horses. "Y'all doing good, Mister Dalton?" "Yes, thanks Zeke," he hollered back. For a split second, Sawyer caught a glimpse of Sadie. With his heart pumping like a race horse, he knew that they just had to be together again.

T he Hat Shoppe was filled with visitors, talking and laughing as they sipped on lemonade and caught up on the town news. "Yes, Mallory is being trained by Mister Dalton over at Lickety-Split Stables." said Miss Hannah. "Though she has been around horses all her life, this is her first derby."

"Did you hear that?" said Buddy. **"Mallory and Sadie are over at the stables where Zeke and Sawyer work."**

Skipper and Brady giggled with excitement, **"Surely they will see each other again!"**

Ring, Ring, Ring...

"Hello, A New Hattitude, Miss BeeDee speaking. How can I help you?"
"Oh no...really, how did it happen? Oh, dear... Ok, call me later."
Click!

"Mister Tanner," said Miss BeeDee, "Sadie is lost. The wind blew her off Mallory's head and they can't find her. Hannah said that Mallory is so upset that she wants to quit the derby."

"You better call Zeke right away!" said Mister Tanner.

Mister Tom Jenkins was the manager at the stables and was very fond of Zeke. When Zeke told Tom about Mallory's hat, he immediately offered to help. **"Ok, here's the plan,"** he said. **"Miss Hannah said they were on the old Town Road when Mallory noticed it missing. Let's start there."**

Zeke and Mister Tom jumped on their horses and headed down the long driveway from Lickety-Split Stables. Sawyer held tight to Zeke's head. As they approached the old Town Rd, Tom stopped and looked around. Sawyer noticed a flower on the ground from Sadie's hat, but Zeke did not see it. Sawyer wiggled back and forth and slid off Zeke's head, floating to the ground right next to the flower.

"Whaaat?" Said Zeke, and he bent down to pick up the hat. **"Hey Tom, he said, I think this is a flower from Mallory's hat. This is where it must have flown off her head."** They searched and searched the whole area but soon the sun was setting and they were exhausted, so they headed home for supper.

14

Meanwhile, feeling lonely and sad, Sadie was stuck in a briar patch at the edge of Old Stone Creek. "Ouch," she winced, **"these prickers are sharp."** She wiggled and wiggled and finally dropped to the ground. **"What now?"** she thought. **"No one will ever find me here."**

Suddenly, a brisk wind picked her up and swirled her around. She landed in a nearby field next to the Old Town Road, where she sat, hoping that someone might see her. But the wind was strong and she was twirled around up in the air until the wind stopped and she drifted down, landing on a large tumbleweed. Gusts of wind sent the tumbleweed bouncing down the dirt road. **"Wheeeee!! This is kind of fun,"** she thought, hoping to get closer to one of the farmhouses as she passed by.

The wind roared and a cloud of dust swept in behind her. Whoosh!! Up, up, up she went, higher and higher, until the wind shifted again, and then she drifted down, side-to-side, back and forth until she finally was swept through the open doors of an abandoned barn. As the dust settled around her, there was a flash of light. Boom!! Lightning, then thunder, and the rain started pouring down.

The next morning, Sadie (a bit disheveled) heard the sounds of children playing outside of the barn. They were playing hide and seek. A little girl dashed into the barn and headed toward the pile of hay in the back. She saw Sadie and picked her up as she continued running. Crouched down behind the haystack, the little girl put on the hat. **"This will be my hat from now on!"**

Sitting at the breakfast table with Sadie on her head, Emily was eating a stack of flap jacks and bacon. **"Where did that hat come from?"** inquired Miss Claire, her Mom. **"...the old abandoned barn on Barker's farm,"** said Emily, **"found it laying in the dirt."**

(Before Miss Claire could respond...) **"I need to go into town for supplies,"** said Mister Joe, Emily's Dad. **"You girls coming with me?"** Emily jumped down from her chair and sped to the door. Miss Claire took off her apron and followed behind.

The three headed into The Broken Spoke General Store. The young boy behind the counter was wearing an oversized sombrero from the Hat Shoppe named Santiago. It shaded his face from the hot sun when he was carrying supplies from the shed. He saw Sadie on Emily's head but was too far away to catch her attention. Emily and Miss Hannah wandered over to the front corner of the store to look at the toys. Mister Joe bought ten pounds of feed for the pigs and some nails to repair the fence.

Emily and her Mom followed Mister Joe into the Hat Shoppe to drop off two pairs of jeans to be patched. Miss BeeDee was in the back of the shop and called, "Be right out". He turned to Miss Claire and said, "I have to go to the Blacksmith after this so why don't you take Emily to the Sweet Shop and I'll meet you there."

As Emily and her Mom left the shop, Bridgette called out, "Sadie, come back!" A second later, Miss BeeDee appeared and greeted Mister Joe. "Aww, they just missed her," said Darby. "Sadie was in the shop and they didn't see her, whined Buddy." "At least we know she's ok," said Cody. "Yeah, she's safe," chuckled Skipper.

Later that day, Zeke and Mister Tom were at the counter in the General Store buying some feed and a couple of new horse blankets. "She was here," Santiago blurted out to Sawyer. "I saw Sadie! A little girl was wearing her." "What was her name?

Where did they go?" said Sawyer anxiously. "I don't know," said Santiago. "Sadie never got close enough for me to find out." Sawyer's eyes started to tear with disappointment.

The Hat Shoppe was buzzing as usual when Zeke and Mister Tom walked in. Miss BeeDee was all smiles when she saw them, especially Sawyer. Buzzing with excitement, the hats shouted out to Sawyer. **"We saw Sadie, said Parker, the Policeman, she was in the store. A little girl was wearing her."** Bonnie piped in **"Miss BeeDee was in the back and she missed them."** Sawyer let out a sigh, **"Yes, Santiago said they were in the General Store also, but he didn't get to talk to her."**

Mister Dalton (standing alongside the mirror) was admiring how handsome he looked with his new hat, Cody, the Cowboy.

The Jackson twins, Will and Wyatt were dancing around the shop, wearing their new hats, Buddy the Beanie, and Skipper the Sailor, while older sister Evelyn, was feeling very pretty and so grown up, wearing Bridgette the Beret.

Mister Bill Jackson laughed, **"Never seen the young-uns' so excited before. I think your hats have magic powers, Miss BeeDee, because every owner is so happy. As for me, I've got a new Hattitude!"**

Miss BeeDee leaned over her sewing machine with straw sections in her hand and colored fabric draped over her lap. **"Now what am I going to name you?"** she thought. Well...I see beautiful colors and lots of flowers so that's where we will start, and then we will know your name. And tomorrow, we will introduce you to your new owner, Mallory.

The sun was shining in the bright blue sky. It was a big day in Bluemont, Kentucky; **the 3rd annual Durango Derby!** The stands were filling up as the excited crowds of kids, parents, grandmas, horse trainers, dogs, cats and other animals made their way to the racetrack. Miss BeeDee and Mister Tanner knew that it was also a "reunion-day" for many of her precious hat creations.

Mallory was wearing a colorful new Miss BeeDee creation named Emma, and was ready for her first race. She loved the new hat but still missed Sadie. Zeke, and Mister Dalton led Mallory's horse around the practice ring, listening for instructions from the announcer, while Sawyer and Cody joked with each other. Emily, wearing Sadie, and her parents entered through the main gate and headed over to the horse stalls to look at the animals.

Zeke caught a glimpse of a small girl with Mallory's hat on her head. He tried to make his way over to her, but the crowd was too big and he lost her. **"Sadie, he thought, now had a new life with this little girl."**

Miss Hannah and Maddie stood up in the stands next to the announcer and Theodore. Santiago sat atop the head of the boy from the General Store, and Brady had a great view on the head of the town Blacksmith.

The race was wonderful. Everyone had a great time. As the crowd moved from the track out into the fields, Miss Hannah, Mallory's Mom saw Sadie on the head of little Emily. She ran up to her and asked her where she got it. **"I found it in an abandoned barn next to Old Town Road."**

Sweetheart, said Miss Hannah. Do you know Miss BeeDee? **"Yes,"** said Emily, shyly. **"Well Miss BeeDee made that hat and it belongs to my daughter Mallory, but one day the wind blew it off her head and she has been looking for it ever since."**

"Oh, I'm sorry," said the little girl. **"I didn't know anyone was looking for it."** Miss Claire stood listening as Miss Mallory said, **"May I introduce you and your Mom to my daughter Mallory?"** Shaking her head with approval, Miss Claire reached out her hand to Emily and they headed back to the racetrack.

Mallory and Zeke were talking when Miss Hannah walked over. **"This is Emily and Miss Claire, her Mom,"** said Miss Hannah. Without a word, Emily took Sadie off her head and handed it to Mallory. Mallory couldn't believe her eyes. **"Ohh...she took a deep breath and didn't know what to say. "I found it in an abandoned barn at Barker's farm,"** said Emily, **"I didn't know it was yours." "Thank you so much,"** said Mallory, as she bent down and held the new bonnet in front of Emily. **"This is Emma,"** she said. **"Would you like her to be yours?"** Tears streamed down Emily's face as she reached for the colorful hat. **"Yes, thank-you"** she said.

Mallory twirled around in circles with a huge smile on her face. Zeke was so happy that he put his arms around her and lifted her in the air shouting, "Woo-hoo!" Sawyer and Sadie's brims touched each other as they repeated each other's names over and over.

Mallory and Zeke held hands as they walked through the field next to the racetrack. Sadie and Sawyer's straps twirled around each other and fell loosely in the back. They smiled at each other, knowing that they would be together forever.

THE END

a New
Hattitude